YOUR KNOWLEDGE HAS VALUE

Bibliographic information published by the German National Library:

The German National Library lists this publication in the National Bibliography; detailed bibliographic data are available on the Internet at http://dnb.dnb.de .

Imprint:

Copyright © 2016 GRIN Verlag, Open Publishing GmbH
Print and binding: Books on Demand GmbH, Norderstedt Germany
ISBN: 978-3-668-21887-1

This book at GRIN:

http://www.grin.com/en/e-book/317400/influence-on-the-children-and-youth-in-the-third-reich-by-national-socialism

Paul Guyet

Influence on the Children and Youth in the Third Reich by National Socialism and Ideologies

GRIN Publishing

GRIN - Your knowledge has value

Since its foundation in 1998, GRIN has specialized in publishing academic texts by students, college teachers and other academics as e-book and printed book. The website www.grin.com is an ideal platform for presenting term papers, final papers, scientific essays, dissertations and specialist books.

Visit us on the internet:

http://www.grin.com/

http://www.facebook.com/grincom

http://www.twitter.com/grin_com

Städtisches Gymnasium Broich
Ritterstraße 21
45479 Mülheim an der Ruhr

Facharbeit

im Grundkurs Geschichte (bilingual)

Influence on the Children and Youth in the Third Reich by National Socialism and Ideologies

Verfasser:	Paul Y. Guyet
Schuljahr:	Q1
Abgabetermin:	15.02.2016

„In unseren Augen muss der deutsche Junge der Zukunft schlank und rank sein, flink wie Windhunde, zäh wie Leder und hart wie Kruppstahl."

Adolf Hitler on September 14th, 1935, in front of 50,000 members of the Hitler Youth in Nürnberg

Table of Contents

1 Introduction

In the time between 1933 and 1945 the National Socialists led by Adolf Hitler reigned in Germany and formed a dictatorship. This time is mainly characterized by the Holocaust and the general racism of Germans in the Third Reich.

The following term paper deals with the life of children and youth in the Third Reich. Influenced by the National Socialism and Adolf Hitler's ideologies of a "perfect German", the youth was taught racism and Nazi ideologies. You can say, they were brainwashed and they were educated to fight for their country in wars. The adolescent believed they were doing the right thing by joining youth organizations and going to Nazi elite schools, such as the Adolf-Hitler-School. What the youth was taught in those establishments back then seems unconceivable to us today. The young people were educated to become racists and warriors. They were even convinced that it was good to be that kind of person and Germany would be proud of them.

The central question I want to treat with this term paper is: How was it possible to control the mind of the German People and leading them to go to war?

2 Hitler's Way to Power

After Germany lost the World War One in 1918, Anton Drexler established the German Workers' Party[1] in the Weimar Republic. Headed by Adolf Hitler, the party was the leading force between 1933 and 1945. Hitler established an unrestricted dictatorship in place of the parliamentary democracy of the Weimar Republic[2].[3] The Third Reich was founded and year by year the party, now called the NSDAP[4], gained more control over schools and media to influence the German people. The National Socialists more or less controlled the people's mind. Hitler had probably imagined his way to autocracy to be more difficult. In fact, he managed to rise almost effortless.

2.1 Ideologies and Aims

The National Socialist ideology can be described by four keywords: *anti-Semitism*, *racial ideology*, *habitat ideology*, and the idea of the national community with the *leadership principle*.[5]

Anti-Semitism is the hostility to Jews. It is the first thing coming to people's mind when thinking of the time of National Socialism in Germany. Approximately six million Jews lost their life during the cruel time of the Holocaust. The reason for the hatred against the Jewish people was more or less religious. Hitler blamed the Jews for Jesus' death. They were depicted as evil and Hitler wanted them to

---

[1] German: Deutsche Arbeiterpartei, DAP

[2] existing since 1871

[3] compare (Mommsen, 2005, S. 19)

[4] German: Nationalsozialistische Deutsche Arbeiterpartei (NSDAP), English: National Socialist German Workers' Party

[5] compare (Die NS-Zeit - die nationalsozialistische Ideologie, 2016)

suffer. Besides being absurd to let innocent people suffer for what happened over 1900 years ago, we nowadays know that it hadn't been the responsibility of the Jews, but the former Romans because they had handed down the death sentence to Jesus.

Based on the Social Darwinism[1], the *racial ideology* was Hitler's main ideology. It said, that the people should be divided into "Master Races", of which the German race was considered as "the best", and the "inferior" races, consisting of non-German races and people with disabilities. The Social Darwinism also led to the *habitat ideology*. In Hitler's opinion, the Germans were the "best" race and therefore should have more claim on territory, so he intended to expand the Third Reich eastbound. His long-term aim was to dominate the whole world.

The *leadership principle* describes the politic system "from top to bottom", which means that Hitler was in command and the people had to follow. He extended his power by filling management positions with National Socialists, so they would definitely obey his orders without questioning.[2]

To sum it up, Hitler's aim was to gain world domination by building a better "Master Race". He wanted to annihilate the "inferior" races to gain habitat for the "Master Race", the pure Germans. His thinking was based on Charles Darwin's theory of evolution, which he transferred to humans (Social Darwinism). The Germans were thrilled by National Socialism because it apparently combined two ideologies: national strength (nationalism) and a social state (socialism).[3]

---

[1] named after Charles Darwin, English naturalist and geologist, best known for his contributions to evolutionary theory

[2] compare (Kamusella, 2016)

[3] compare (Lerntippsammlung, 2016)

2.2 Educational Work of Hitler

Hitler knew, he could influence the people with propagandas, scare them through terror, or dazzle them by economic and political success, thus convincing the folk to vote and support him. But he could never "delete" the people's memories of the time before the National Socialism. Because of this, Hitler wanted to get control of the youth. To reach this goal, he had to control the education as well and this is exactly what he did.

In 1936 already 96% of all educators[1] belonged to the National Socialist Teachers League[2]. This league of teachers for public schools taught the youth ideologies and principles set by Hitler. His main principle was not the mere "filling" of the children's heads with a great deal of knowledge, but to shape a healthy and well trained body. Secondly followed the education of mental abilities.

The required culturing of an optimal healthy body was implemented in youth organizations, in schools, and since 1934 in about 43,000 sport clubs. The curriculum for mental education included mainly to fill the whole lessons with the pseudo derivation of the Third Reich from the heroic spirit and the idea of the leadership. The aim was to fascinate the youth and to arouse the desire to join the "Wehrmacht"[3]. Hitler was shown as a hero in school in terms of being the leader of the Nazi "movement". Biology for example was filled with racial and heredity teachings to instill racism or hate against not "pureblooded" humans.

> "Die gesamte Bildungs- und Erziehungsarbeit des völkischen Staates muß ihre Krönung darin finden, daß sie den Rassesinn und das Rassegefühl instinkt- und verstandgemäß im Herz und Gehirn der ihr anvertrauten Jugend hinein brennt. Es soll kein Knabe und kein Mädchen die Schule verlassen ohne zur letzten Erkenntnis über die Notwendigkeit und das Wesen der Blutreinheit geführt worden zu sein." (Hitler, 1925, S. 475 f.)

---

[1] teachers, professors, etc.

[2] German: Nationalsozialistischer Lehrerbund

[3] The unified armed forces of Nazi Germany

Beginning with Potsdam, Plön, and Köslin on April 19th 1933, the regime started building "Nationalsozialistische Erziehungsanstalten"[1] directed and managed by Bernhard Rust (1883-1945)[2]. Year by year more and more schools were built. In 1937 "Adolf-Hitler-Schools" were founded and built from then on. These schools should arise to compete with other educational institutes in every NSDAP "Gau"[3]. Selected students from the age of twelve were trained there for a period of six years to become the leader's offspring, of which a quarter afterwards continued their education on the "Ordensburgen"[4] for future elite.[5]

---

[1] English: "National Socialist educational institutions" → Napola

[2] minister of education

[3] district

[4] elite school for physical- and character education of junior leaders

[5] compare (Brechtken, 2004, S. 75 ff.)

3 Everyday Life of Children and Youth

Most of today's adolescents in Germany think they live a normal life. But what exactly is "a normal life"? When thinking of a normal life today, you think of going to school, doing your homework, pursuing hobbies, meeting friends, and so on. During the National Socialism it was a bit different. The childhood and especially the youth in the Third Reich is not comparable to the everyday life of today's adolescents. The young people of the Third Reich didn't have a chance for free decisions and individuality. Their life was controlled and regulated by the Nazi regime. They belonged to their "leader", Adolf Hitler, and were educated according to Nazi regulations. School was adapted to Nazi ideologies and National Socialist youth organizations became mandatory for all adolescents aged between 10 to 18 years, so Hitler could be sure that the next generation corresponds to his ideal.[1]

3.1 The Hitler Youth

The Hitler Youth was the youth organization of the Third Reich. Besides the schools, it was the most important way to educate the children and youth in the sense of Nazi ideology. With the foundation in July 3rd/4th 1926, it was only a small National Socialist Youth Movement in the Weimar Republic. But since the Nazis became the leading power in 1933, the Hitler Youth became the one solitary youth organization. Every other youth organization had been prohibited. At first, a membership was no obligation, but you had to expect disadvantages in further life. You were not allowed to join a sports club, nor was it easy to get a job. The later obligation led to an increase of from about 108 thousand to 8.7 million members[2]. As there was a total population of 8,870 thousand ten to 18-

---

[1] compare (Sand, 2016)

[2] including the League of German Girls

year-old, about 98% of German adolescents were controlled by the National Socialist's youth organization.

The Hitler Youth, which is of course named after the head of the NSDAP, Adolf Hitler, had its main task to prepare the adolescent Germans between the age of 10 and 18 years for war. To "build" the "perfect soldier", they were taught obedience, various commands, comradeship, discipline and self-sacrifice. With the end of the second World War in April/May 1945, the Hitler Youth had ceased to exist. On October 10th 1945 the youth organization, along with every other organization founded and led by the Nazi party, was finally prohibited.

3.1.1 Organization and Structure

The organization of the Hitler Youth was subordinated to the supreme leadership of the Sturmabteilung[1] since May 1st 1931 and was strictly hierarchical. After the SA as well as the Hitler Youth had been prohibited in April 1932, the organization became more or less a forbidden youth movement. With the election of the Nazi party, the nomination of the new Reichsjugendführer[2] led to the control over the Hitler Youth by the NSDAP.

The adolescents were divided by age, region and gender of course. Boys aged between 10 and 14 years could join the Youth every year on Hitler's birthday, April 20th. From that moment on they belonged to the "Deutsches Jungvolk"[3] (DJ), whereas the 14- to 18-years-old formed the actual Hitler Youth. To become part of the Hitler Youth, the "Jungvolk" had to pass the "Pimpfenprobe"[4]. This test consisted of theoretical questions about Germany and the Third Reich plus sporting challenges. It included tasks like a 70-meter run in less than 15

---

[1] armed and uniformed branch of the NSDAP (SA)

[2] (English: Reich youth leader) Baldur von Schirach, later (since 1940) Artur Axmann

[3] English: young people of Germany

[4] English: test for whippersnappers

seconds, a long jump of 3.50 meters, rounders throwing of at least 25 meters, a one-minute stoppage of breath, a participation in a one-day trip, knowledge of the structure and the leadership of the "DJ-Fähnlein"[1], knowledge of German songs like the Horst Wessel Song[2] and the Hitler Youth's banner song, and knowledge of the "Schwertworte des Hitlerjungen"[3,4]

Furthermore, the youth was also divided into about 10 units which were specialized for several interests and talents, for example the marine, the motor, the news, or the patrol duty Hitler Youth. (Jugend 1918-1945, 2016)

There were several ranks building the hierarchy of the Hitler Youth. The highest rank was the "Reichsjugendführer", which was occupied by Baldur von Schirach, an enthusiastic supporter and member of the NSDAP.

3.1.2 Joining Incentives

Although it has been compulsory to join the Hitler Youth, most of the adolescents were keen to finally be able to join with an age of 10 years. But why? What attracted the young people to join the youth organization of National Socialism?

This enthusiasm was the result of Hitler's and the NSDAP's talent for propagandas, to represent all these Nazi ideologies as positive, as desirable and worthwhile. The youth was very important for Hitler, because he wanted to have a next generation formed completely to meet his requirements. For the individual young person, this often meant to finally get awarded a long-awaited attention and responsibility, because the now uniformed child or young person was

---

[1] name for third biggest unit of the „Deutsches Jungvolk" (about 140 boys)

[2] anthem of the Nazi Party from 1930 to 1945

[3] (English: sword words of Hitler Youth) hardness, bravery, loyalty, attitude, truth, camaraderie, honor

[4] compare (Deutsches Jungvolk - Wikipedia, 2016)

shown respect. Also many children and youths in the Third Reich wanted to be part of something. This has not really changed much over time. Nowadays a lot of children are members in sport clubs for example. Playing in a team is more fun than playing alone. This is exactly what the Hitler Youth offered. Propaganda marches and parades, trips, outdoor games, and sociable camp life were made for bigger groups of teenagers and were very popular. The youth was taught discipline by games and fun. On the other side, another big reason for many adolescents to join the Hitler Youth was the fear of having disadvantages in further life. Persons who did not join the Hitler Youth had more difficulties to get a job, because every company was controlled by the NSDAP and so they would not hire these people.

3.1.3 Educational Focus

In contrast to the education in school in Nazi Germany, the education in the Hitler Youth concentrated on physical training and "building" the perfect soldier. At least two times a week they had official duty. Every Wednesday a social evening took place, where the adolescents listened to propaganda radio, sang songs, or had ideological training. Every Saturday members of the Hitler Youth joined, instead of school, sports lessons including military training. Since 1934 the SS[1] got increasingly more influence on the Hitler Youth and so they recruited boys with an age of 17 years or above, who did well in the military training, for the SS elite unit. Furthermore, they organized weekend trips twice a month for the Hitler Youth to train obedience and comradeship and to increase their independence and separation from the parental home. In addition to these obligations, there were special services the adolescents had to follow, like participation in rallies, advertising campaigns, appeals, and celebrations. All of these duties were intentional to turn young people into a soldier. You can say that Hit-

---

[1] "Schutzstaffel" (English: protection squadron); major paramilitary organization under the NSDAP

ler's main aim for the education in the Hitler Youth was to prepare the adolescents for an upcoming war without letting them really know.

3.1.4 Impact on the Wehrmacht

"Was sind wir? Pimpfe! Was wollen wir werden? Soldaten!"[1] was one of the slogans the youth heard over and over again in order to make them look forward to finally join the Wehrmacht. One of Hitler's main aims was to prepare the next generation for an upcoming war. According to Darwin's Theory of Evolution's conversion on humans, Hitler thought that Germany had been entitled to expand, because the Germans were the "best" and "strongest" race. But to expand the "German Reich" he needed an army first: the "Wehrmacht". And that's what he intended to build up with the Hitler Youth: as perfectly trained soldiers for war, the youth was optimally prepared for the Wehrmacht. They had to complete mandatory military service of two years since March 16th 1935, but everything a soldier needed, the adolescents had already been taught in the Hitler Youth. Apart from discipline and obedience they learned the handling of rifles and grenades as well as basic military skills such as map reading and being exposed to physical strains.

To summarize, we can make a note to the point that the Hitler Youth had a huge influence on the military because it simply included the preparation of young men for soldiers of the Wehrmacht. Adolescents had to join the army for at least two years, starting with an age of 19 at the latest. Most of them even wanted to stay in the Wehrmacht because of Hitler's conviction for patriotism.

3.2 Rejection and Resistance

Despite the increasing pressure of the NSDAP, a growing group of young people opposed the National Socialism. This had several reasons. A large number

---

[1] (Kater, 2005, S. 30) English: „What are we? Whippersnappers! What do we want to be? Soldiers!"

of the youths wanted a freer youth culture or just pure adventure, others continued the traditions of the youth organizations that were prohibited in 1933, and again others rejected the state for religious reasons. Although most of them liked the Hitler Youth once, the resistance intensified from the moment the youth organization mainly focused on military preparation.

Non-participation in the Hitler Youth service, maintaining traditional organizations[1], refusal of National Socialists' standards, or partly active resistance[2], for example, were the youth's ways to show their resistance. In "illegal" youth organizations such as the "Weiße Rose" or the "Swing-Jugend", resistive young people united. These groups were critically observed by the National Socialists, and were systematically prosecuted and punished. Individual youths who attempted to do "anti-propaganda" had to expect to be prosecuted and to face death penalty.[3]

3.3 The League of German Girls

Besides the Hitler Youth every other youth organization was prohibited. But there was another youth organization of the NSDAP, namely the League of German Girls[4], the girls' wing of the Hitler Youth, which was established in 1930. Like the Hitler Youth, the League was divided into two sections: the "Jungmädel" for girls with an age of 10 to 14 years and the actual "League of German Girls" for the 14- to 18-year-old. Additionally, there was the "Faith and

---

[1] For example, youth organizations of the SPD or KPD

[2] For example, sabotage, leaflet distribution

[3] compare (Lichte, 2016)

[4] German: Bund Deutscher Mädel

Beauty Society"[1] which was voluntary and open to girls between the ages of 17 and 21.

Similar to the boys, the activities of the League of German Girls were excursions, hiking, and marches followed by campfire cooking and joint singing. But as the promotion of strength, endurance, and toughness of the boys was the main focus of the Hitler Youth, the girls did rhythmic gymnastics for developing grace. Instead of strength and roughness they trained to impress men over the outward appearance. Ideologies, which were drummed into the girls, were for example, "the more children you get the better wife you are", or if they would send their children in the Nazi youth organizations, they would gain a higher prestige.

> „Die Gleichberechtigung der Frau besteht darin, daß sie in den ihr von der Natur bestimmten Lebensgebieten jene Hochschätzung erfährt, die ihr zukommt […] Auch die deutsche Frau hat ihr Schlachtfeld: Mit jedem Kinde, das sie der Nation zur Welt bringt, kämpft sie ihren Kampf für die Nation." (Klose, 1982, S. 275-276)

All in all, you can say that the League of German Girls differed a lot from the Hitler Youth. While the Hitler Youth's aim was to prepare the boys for the Wehrmacht, the League of German Girls' objective was to prepare the girls for a life as a housewife. That's why the activities were different and why there was no test after the "Jungmädelbund". The supervision of the NSDAP and the structure were the only things they had in common.[2]

---

[1] German: Werk Glaube und Schönheit

[2] compare (Bund Deutscher Mädel - Wikipedia, 2016)

4 Conclusion

After the defeat of Germany in World War One in 1918, the German Workers' Party was founded. With their leader Adolf Hitler, the party became the leading force from 1933 to 1945. The National Socialists followed several ideologies, namely the idea of the national community with the leadership principle, habitat ideology, anti-Semitism and racial ideology. Consequently, Hitler wanted to systematically eliminate every person in Germany, which did not correspond to these ideologies. Innocent people such as people with disabilities or people of other races had to suffer from this.

Hitler's biggest aim was to take control over the youth to secure the future of the German dictatorship and to expand the army of the Wehrmacht. To accomplish his goal, Hitler founded the Hitler Youth. It was basically the only youth organization of the Third Reich because every other organization was prohibited by the NSDAP. Boys with an age of ten could join the "Deutsches Jungvolk" and were promoted to the actual Hitler Youth with 14 if they passed a specific test ("Pimpfenprobe"). In the Hitler Youth they were trained according to Hitler's ideal; they had, for example, race studies in biology. Moreover, they had physical training including military exercises such as handling weapons or joint marches. In this way they already had their military training completed before the age of 18 and thus they could join the Wehrmacht right after the Hitler Youth.

The girl's wing of the Hitler Youth was called League of German Girls and had more or less the same structure. From 10 to 14 years, the girls belonged to the "Jungmädel" and after that (aged between 14 and 18 years) to the actual League of German Girls. The objective of this organization was to prepare the girls for a life as a housewife. They were educated in cooking and everything they needed to know about birth and babies. But they were also, as well as the boys, taught the Nazi ideologies in order to be able to pass these on to the next generation when raising their kids

The central question raised in the introduction of this term paper on page 4 was: "How was it possible to control the mind of the German People and leading them to go to war?". In my opinion the simple answer is that Hitler was a genius when it came to convincing people. The lost World War One was very handy for him as well. The German people had poor prospects after the painful defeat in war, and Hitler promised them a better life and a better Germany. The people began to like him, the NSDAP became the leading power, and by the time almost every German citizen followed Hitler blindly. From then on it just needed a breeze to turn them into patriots. Hitler started to control the youth through the Hitler Youth. He taught them to fight for their fatherland and to follow his commands. As even the nursery school was controlled by the National Socialists, children were influenced by Nazi ideologies since their first years of life.

From today's point of view, you could probably not imagine at all something like the National Socialism to happen again. But looking at the movement of the contemporary organization of the Islamic State (IS) you can realize some similarities. This organization follows ideologies as well and influences the children and youth with special forms of education, like Hitler did with the Hitler Youth. A further comparison and detailed treatment of this topic would, however, go beyond the scope of this term paper.

5 Literature and List of Sources

Barth, R. (2004). *Deutsche Geschichte - Basiswissen zum Mitreden*. Bindlach: Loewe Verlag GmBH.

Brechtken, M. (2004). *Die nationalsozialistische Herrschaft 1933-1939*. Darmstadt: Wissenschaftliche Buchgesellschaft.

Hitler, A. (1925). *Mein Kampf*. o. O.: Mein Kampf.

Jugend 1918-1945. (07. 02 2016). *Jugend 1918-45 - Der HJ-Dienst*. Von Jugend 1918-45: http://www.jugend1918-1945.de/thema.aspx?s=5373&m=3448 abgerufen

Jugend 1918-1945. (01. 02 2016). *Jugend 1918-45 - Die Organisation der HJ*. Von Jugend 1918-45: http://www.jugend1918-1945.de/thema.aspx?s=5371&m=3448&open=5371 abgerufen

Jugend 1918-1945. (02. 02 2016). *Jugend 1918-45 - HJ-Gesetz und Jugenddienstpflicht*. Von Jugend 1918-45: http://www.jugend1918-1945.de/thema.aspx?s=5380&m=3448&v=5380 abgerufen

Kamusella. (04. 02 2016). *Die NS-Zeit - die nationalsozialistische Ideologie*. Von Kamusella: http://kamusella.de/luise/schule/geschichte/abiwissen/4nszt/402_ns-ideologie.html abgerufen

Kater, M. H. (2005). *Hitler-Jugend*. Darmstadt.

Klose, W. (1982). *Generation im Gleichschritt - Die Hitlerjugend*. München.

Lerntippsammlung. (04. 02 2016). *Ideologien im Nationalsozialismus - Referat, Hausaufgabe, Hausarbeit*. Von Lerntippsammlung: http://www.lerntippsammlung.de/Ideologien-im-Nationalsozialismus.html abgerufen

Lichte, M. (09. 02 2016). *Der Widerstand Jugendlicher gegen den Nationalsozialismus.* Von trend.infopartisan: http://www.trend.infopartisan.net/trd0699/t160699.html abgerufen

Liepach, M. (2001). *Nationalsozialismus und Zweiter Weltkrieg.* Freising: Stark Verlagsgesellschaft mBH.

Mommsen, H. (2005). Der "Führerstaat". In C. Stern, & I. Brodersen, *Eine Erdbeere für Hitler* (S. 19-57). Frankfurt am Main: S. Fischer Verlag GmbH.

Sand, M. (07. 02 2016). *Wie lebten Kinder und Jugendliche im Nationalsozialismus?* Von Wannewitz: http://www.wannewitz.de/Kurse/zk13/Jugend%20Nationalsozialismus.htm abgerufen

Wikipedia. (09. 02 2016). *Bund Deutscher Mädel - Wikipedia.* Von Wikipedia: https://de.wikipedia.org/wiki/Bund_Deutscher_M%C3%A4del#cite_note-1 abgerufen

Wikipedia. (07. 02 2016). *Deutsches Jungvolk - Wikipedia.* Von Wikipedia: https://de.wikipedia.org/wiki/Deutsches_Jungvolk#Pimpfenprobe abgerufen

Wikipedia. (31. 01 2016). *Hitlerjugend - Wikipedia.* Von Wikipedia: https://de.wikipedia.org/wiki/Hitlerjugend abgerufen